MONSTER POETRY

Creepy Creations

Edited By Andy Porter

First published in Great Britain in 2023 by:

YoungWriters® Est. 1991

Young Writers
Remus House
Coltsfoot Drive
Peterborough
PE2 9BF
Telephone: 01733 890066
Website: www.youngwriters.co.uk

All Rights Reserved
Book Design by Ashley Janson
© Copyright Contributors 2023
Softback ISBN 978-1-80459-835-1

Printed and bound in the UK by BookPrintingUK
Website: www.bookprintinguk.com
YB0560H

Foreword

Young Writers was created in 1991 with the express purpose of promoting and encouraging creative writing. Each competition we create is tailored to the relevant age group, giving each child the inspiration and incentive to create their own piece of writing, whether it's a poem or a short story. We truly believe that seeing it in print gives pupils a sense of achievement and pride in their work and themselves.

Our latest competition, Monster Poetry, focuses on uncovering the different techniques used in poetry and encouraging pupils to explore new ways to write a poem. Using a mix of imagination, expression and poetic styles, this anthology is an impressive snapshot of the inventive, original and skilful writing of young people today. These poems showcase the creativity and talent of these budding new writers as they learn the skills of writing, and we hope you are as entertained by them as we are.

Harry King (9)	62
Isla Harris (8)	64
Katie Norris	65
Skye Mordecai (9)	66
George (8)	67
Marla O'Connor (8)	68
Sophie Egan (8)	69
Toby Bates (9)	70
Gracie Griffiths	71
Georgiana Dando	72
Dylan O'Connor (9)	73
Mollie Griffiths	74
Scarlett Powell-Bright (8)	75
Noah Williams (8)	76
Ruby Hill (8)	77
Jack Stevens (8)	78
Bailey Williams (8)	79
Isaac Edwards (8)	80

Long Whatton CE Primary School, Loughborough

Rocco Staples (8)	81
Edith Macfarlane (9)	82
Logan Dodoo (8)	85
Keigan Fearn (8)	86
Tessa Bradley (8)	88
Thomas Robertshaw (9)	90
Lauren Winter (8)	92
Billy Steel (9)	93
Joshua Bown (8)	94
Jack Mayfield (9)	95
Izzy Mantey (8)	96
Maisy Chadaway (9)	97
Harper Bowley (8)	98
Oliver Claye (8)	99
Nate Sharples (9)	100
Lily Winter (8)	101
Evie Claye (8)	102
Tom Gaskell (8)	103
Layla Biddulph (8)	104
Lilah Afonso (8)	105

Longmeadow Primary School, Broadwater

Casey Elam (10)	106
Indi Hyde (10)	108
Phoebe D (10)	110
Juan Ibe (10)	112
Mia-Lily Whitfield (10)	114
Sienna M (10)	115
Jazzy Joseph (10)	116
Patricia Chiaga (10)	118
Victoria P (9)	119
Ronnie Hull (10)	120
Lacey Bradshaw (10)	121
Maja D (10)	122
Lara Senior (10)	123
Riley Bartlett (10)	124
Amariah Williams (9)	125
Evie Gray (9)	126
Holly W (10)	127
Esme B (10)	128
Alexis S (10)	129
Mia A (10)	130
Jesseca C (10)	131
Ella D (9)	132
Tommy T (10)	133
Riley Barmby (10)	134
Jude Smith (10)	135
Evie-Mae L (10)	136

The Poems

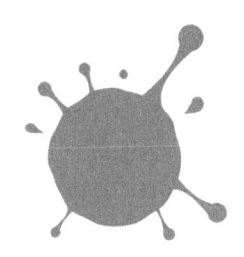

Scaly's Friendship

A female monster named Scaly
Had no friends except Jimmy
He was always kind to her
When others were not
One day she saved the most popular monster *ever*
Her name was Taylor
She was so tall, so thin, so *orange*
She was so grateful, she squealed in joy
"Okay, you are *so* nice and sweet Scaly,
Let's be friends"
They were not just friends, they were *besties*
So she became popular like Taylor
But she didn't forget her best friend ever, Jimmy
She became more and more popular
She didn't forget
She played in a movie, she didn't forget
She got a *million* more friends
But she *still* didn't forget, she swore
She would never forget.

Annie Mayo (11)
Beetham CofE Primary School, Milnthorpe

Yabaha

A rider went into the deep dark wood
Never expecting to come back
Pulling up their cloak hood
They followed along the track.

The further they got
The more they heard the voices
They just didn't want to get caught
But then came more noises.

"Yabaha, Yabaha, Yabaha," came from the trees
The rider turned around in a circle
They got hit in the head and landed on their knees
They were in very big trouble.

When they awoke
They were being spun around
In their face, there was lots of smoke
Then there was a sound.

Like a little mouse
And in the distance a tiny house
The creatures were slicing vegetables on boards.

The juices squirted into the rider's face
They squirmed and wriggled to get free
The tiny creature then grabbed a mace
The rider had to flee!

They broke out of the ropes
Run, run, run, go run out of the woods
Up and down the slopes
Pulling up their hood.

The rider escaped the terror of the Fijig Bijig
And lived to tell the tale
No one saw the Fijig Bijig again but knew it was still there
"Yabaha, Yabaha, Yabaha," came from the tree.

Lily-Ann Whittaker
Beetham CofE Primary School, Milnthorpe

Charlie

Charlie the monster is very cute,
He loves music very much,
But he doesn't like the flute,
When his parents make him he hides in a bush.

Charlie used to live in a small village called Musicton,
Till he moved to a town Flutevill,
He had to leave his best friend John,
He missed his pal so he fell ill.

Charlie decided he wanted to go away,
He settled on a tall mountain with snow,
After what felt like ages he found a sleigh,
At the bottom, he found a photo.

Charlie thought, *What could it be?*
A photo of what?
A cosy valley,
With a load of chestnut.

Charlie followed the magical map,
To a town called Rock'n'pop,
He walked into a huge clap,
Then he found John on a treetop.

Charlie in his shorts of green,
Found his place to call home,
He and his pal sat and ate jellybeans,
In the place they could roam.

Lucy Johnson
Beetham CofE Primary School, Milnthorpe

The Monster Who Loves Water

Three, two, one, off we went,
Into the stars, we flew,
I saw the Earth down below,
As I landed a monster said, "*Boo!*"

I met a monster from the planet Foxalite,
It was very cute,
His teeth were sharp, pointy and white,
He was wearing red rain boots.

Three, two, one, off we went,
Back down to Earth, we came,
I brought him to my home,
I asked, "What is your name?"

He said his name was Fuggle,
Water was what he loved,
He really liked to snuggle,
His favourite flower was a fox glove.

We played in the water for hours,
We got to know each other,
He said, "I have water powers,"
His favourite food was oysters.

We got out since it was night,
I said, "You are now my pet!"
The round moon was shining bright,
And that's how we became best friends.

Megan Selby (11)
Beetham CofE Primary School, Milnthorpe

The Fear Of The Monsters

In the darkest of dark
In the nightest of night
You feel the fear of the fright
You better sleep tight.

The monsters will be upright
Staring into your eyes
The creak of the bedside
The door scraping the floor.

His breath as cold as the Antarctic ocean
His teeth as sharp as a knife
His blood as hot as lava
His eyes are as red as fire.

He hides in the fear of your nightmare
Eats the daylight out of you
He hornets you day and night
And eats your sweet dreams.

Lucas Hammond
Beetham CofE Primary School, Milnthorpe

Micro Monster

As small as an ant
I can see you
I can hear you
But...
You can't see or hear me.

As fluffy as a dog
I can feel you
I can taste you
But...
You can't feel or taste me.

As bitey as a horsefly
I can spook you
I can hurt you
If...
You hurt me.

As small as an ant
As fluffy as a dog

As bitey as a horsefly
As camouflaged as an octopus.

Catch me if you can...

Alisha Carradus
Beetham CofE Primary School, Milnthorpe

Monster From Mars

There was a monster that came from Mars
All the way amongst the stars
But one day a disaster happened
She fell overboard from her space bird Zapened
As she fell to Earth
She landed in Perth
It was so beautiful she wanted to stay
She came up to me and asked, "Can I play?"
I said, "Yes, what to do?"
She said, "I don't know, how about you?"
We went to the park
And met my friend Mark
Then we went to a factory
And met my friend Malory
We had so many sweets
We fell asleep
And had some wonderful dreams
That were better than they seemed.

Gracie Anderson (8)
Bent Primary School, Lesmahagow

My Monster's Adventure

My monster came from the planet Mars.
He flew through the moon and the stars.
He joined me for the rest of the day.
Until I heard him say, "It's been a nice day but I have to go."

I was quite sad and a little mad.
I told myself it was okay.
But it didn't feel right.
I was upset the full night.
I finally fell asleep but only for an hour.
When I woke up my monster was waiting.

We went on a big adventure to the safari park and also tried sour food.
We had a day but now it's the end.

Matilda Thomson (8)
Bent Primary School, Lesmahagow

We Met The Avengers

My monster loves to travel the world
Join us on our next adventure
Where we meet the Avengers
First, we went to the planet Mars
Where we flew through the stars
We went on the safari
Next, we saw a black Jedi
Then he disappeared
And it looked like he had a beard
Then all the Avengers came
We played lots of games
We started becoming friends
Then they had to go in the end
My monster and I were sad
But they said they would come back
Then we heard a quack
And we laughed
And then we left.

Amber Hamilton (9)
Bent Primary School, Lesmahagow

Travelling Monster

My monster loves to travel the world,
Join us on our next adventure to go see the Avengers.
They're nice but cheeky and sneaky,
Their dream holiday is to go to the jungle.
So we go to the jungle and see lots of animals,
They are so happy, they give big hugs.
We go home for tomorrow's exciting adventure,
A couple of days later, we hear a knock at the door.
It's a DVD so we watch it and it's a video of our holiday.

Lisa Newell (8)
Bent Primary School, Lesmahagow

The Boy And The Monster

This is the tale of a monster and a boy.
They go to the moon to find great joy.
The boy and the monster jump on the moon.
They both fly very high.
Between the stars and the sky.
Next, they go back to the boy's planet.
So they can try a pomegranate.
It isn't the best.
And they start to get depressed.
So they plan a game of chess.
So they aren't as depressed.
They say goodbye.
Then think it is sad.

Jamie Hopkinson (8)
Bent Primary School, Lesmahagow

Me And My Monster

My monster came from the planet Mars,
She flew through the moon and stars.
I woke up in my bed,
One of them said their name was Ned!
We were besties,
We had lots of fun.
We met a pig in a wig,
And she was very friendly!
She followed us the rest of the day,
Just to say, "It's my tea time!"
So I said, "That's okay, see you tomorrow!"
Then we left and snuggled up in bed.

Jessie Wilson (9)
Bent Primary School, Lesmahagow

A Day With My Monster

Fluffy the monster is looking for a friend
Don't worry, this story has a happy end.

Fluffy is very happy
The food she eats is flappy
People don't like her or let her play
It was a school day
She was scared
So she glared.

Another monster came to school
That monster felt like a fool
She saw Fluffy all sad
They came up with a plan
That they would be friends forever.

Rebecca Cosgrove (8)
Bent Primary School, Lesmahagow

A Tale Of A Monster And A Boy

This is the tale of a monster and a boy.
They love to go on missions to find great joy.
This monster and boy love to rob banks.
To steal jewellery in a tank.
They get in trouble all the time.
Even though they do crimes they both give to the poor.
In the end, they're not that bad.
Join them in their next adventure.

Alyssa O'Connor (8)
Bent Primary School, Lesmahagow

Finding A Friend

Rick the monster is looking for a friend
Don't worry, it's a happy end
Rick walks into the classrooms
But no one wants to be his friend
He looks very scary
And makes the teachers wary
But a boy realises he is lonely
And the boy and Rick become best friends.

Arran Murray (8)
Bent Primary School, Lesmahagow

Mike T

Mike T the monster is looking for a friend
Don't worry, this story has a happy end
Mike likes to box in the ring with a fox
After the night he meets a fan
A legend, he was called Dan!
And they became best friends
Then went skydiving.

Harris McBride (8)
Bent Primary School, Lesmahagow

Reality's Reflection

Upon the white-washed walls dripped her blood,
The door started to creak, then came a thud.
A vase smashed and there was a piteous cry,
It was nearly the time for her to die!
The clock ticked away as seconds passed by,
Maybe this murder I should get on and try.
This 'monster' floated into the room,
Amidst the void of darkness and gloom.
Grappling its way towards me,
Then, a resemblance I could see.
This so-called 'monster' was just a girl,
In a torn gown and wearing a string of pearls.
Her face painted in rivers of blood,
Maybe this girl was an omen of good.
Then, she gasped and collapsed to the floor,
Whatever I've done I can't ignore.
This 'monster' was me from the past,
"I am the monster," I say aghast.

Sophia Elizabeth Reed (12)
Ingleby Manor Free School & Sixth Form, Stockton On Tees

All About Opal

M y monster has two tongues, one holds a head and the other holds a gun,
O pal is my monster's name, she smells of coral, but not of fame,
N ight is her time to shine, she loves nature but *hates* to climb its vines,
S topping her won't be fun, if she screams, you have to run,
T ea time is her time to eat, eat her food and she will creep,
E arly morning she will stare, at your picture over there,
R aindrops falling on her face, she sleeps as she's haunting the human race.

O pal teleports through the rain, as you sleep throughout the pain,
P robably right now she's digging your grave, as the Grim Reaper comes to your place,
A s the Reaper comes to you, Opal's eye is on your view,
L ast of all, the Reaper's come, save yourself as you run.

Anousheh Raza (10) & Raza
Lady Royd Primary, Bradford

My Little Monster

My cute little monster is hiding under my chair,
He thinks that I'm a bear!
I'm not going to eat him,
Or beat him.
I just want to play,
He looks like a stray.
I feel kind of bad,
But I don't want to make him sad.
I go up to my room,
Feeling like a fool.
I chased him around the house,
He looked like a poor little mouse.
After thinking and thinking,
I opened the door without blinking.
Standing behind the door,
Stood my little monster paws.
As he leapt into my arms,
I cuddled him and he felt warm.

Eliza Nawaz (10)
Lady Royd Primary, Bradford

Oh Boy, What A Day

My mum and dad bought me a toy
And I named it Oi!
Last night, I slept with my brand new toy called Oi
And oh boy, what did he do?

He ran and ran
Around
He went up and down left and right.

"Argh! It's alive!" Off it went in my room
Finding him without a sound.

Hiding behind my chair he thought
I'm a rare.

No matter what I said
He thought he was a stray wandering around my house
Like there was no other place.

Day after day time to time we
Bonded slowly bonded carefully whatever can
I imagine a little friend came to appear.

After thinking, I finally decided to keep him
Without a struggle, I gasped in shock
And an excited scream let out.

Aliza Hussain (10)
Lady Royd Primary, Bradford

Ice Cream Monster

It's a special day,
Let me tell you something,
I came from a shipping bay,
Created with some bling!

It's my birthday today,
This is gonna be great,
In the month of May,
Let's all celebrate!

My powers include making ice creams,
I've got a wafer cone body, and an ice cream head,
I will be your hero, it will be your dream,
Once a kid said, "I love your ice cream, yummy!"

Today with my ice cream powers,
I'll go to every school in town,
Give them fizzy feelings,
Make every kid make a happy sound!

Today was my birthday,
It was so fun,
It wasn't just the ice cream,
My friends and family made it fun!

Tawassul Jafry (10)
Lady Royd Primary, Bradford

A Day In My Monster Life

I was coming home from school,
After getting called a fool,
I was coming home,
About to give my sister a gnome.

When she got it she was surprised,
Said it would win a prize,
My mom came home,
Said, "Let's see the gnome,"
And said, "Let's place it in front of our home."

My mom called me and said, "What do you want for Easter,
My mini monster?"
"I want a bird feeder to help the birds."
My mom said, "Okay, after we can see our leader."

Anniyah Khan (10)
Lady Royd Primary, Bradford

My Monster Called Rosie

- R osie is so cute and fluffy.
- O range and guava are her favourite fruits.
- S o Rosie is so cute and fluffy.
- I naya is her best friend.
- E njoy, enjoy, enjoy all about my monster called Rosie.

Rosie is so cute and fluffy.
When she combs her hair it turns puffy.
Her favourite fruits are orange and guava.
And she loves her mama and papa.
She loves cream.
And thinks about it in her dreams.
So that is all about my monster called Rosie.
So enjoy, enjoy, enjoy.

Umnia Khan (10)
Lady Royd Primary, Bradford

All About Fizzy

This is Fizzy,
Her best friend is called Lizzy.
She is slimy,
But also tiny.
She is a ghost,
But her favourite food is toast.
She likes to eat,
But strongly dislikes meat.
She is really kind,
And has a great mind.
Her favourite colour is white,
And she loves to play with the kite.
Her second favourite colour is green,
She is never mean.
She likes to read books,
But she always has good luck.

Ayesha Ali (10)
Lady Royd Primary, Bradford

Silly Slimy

My name is Silly Slimy,
I like to be called Slimy,
I love to be happy,
But never angry.

My favourite colour is red,
Because I love to go to bed,
People call me cute,
But sadly I am mute.

I may be silly,
But I am slimy,
And I love myself a strawberry,
And I am very merry.

I don't like school,
Because I am a fool!

My name is Silly Slimy.

Minnah Shahbaz (9)
Lady Royd Primary, Bradford

Blobious The Monster

Down, down, down underground
Lies a town
Whose children go to school
And whose parents go to work
But one stormy night
Everyone wakes up in a fright
A monster comes from up, up, up high
It has jelly hair
Strawberry hands
Butterfly wings
Pancake stomach
Lollipop nose
Unicorn horn
Pink cat ears
Where has this mysterious creature come from?
Outer space?

Khadeejah Osman (10)
Lady Royd Primary, Bradford

Debbie The Devil

Hi, I'm Debbie the Devil!
I have magic but I control its level.
I may look weird and have a different race,
But trust me, I am full of grace!
I like to read which is a good habit,
And my favourite animal is a cute rabbit!
I have a really cute cat,
But I don't know why it likes my hat!
I love the moon at night,
But I can control the sun in daylight!

Menaal Ghahbaz (9)
Lady Royd Primary, Bradford

A Gloomy, Endless Night

A gloomy, endless night
With a gloomy, small monster
But just not any kind of monster
Only the kind of monster that comes in the morning to help you
It also helps you with interacting and dancing
She is shy, also scared, smiley and funny
And she looks scary but don't judge her
She is friendly inside
This is my monster, scary but kind.

Jumaimahussain Jumaimahussain (10)
Lady Royd Primary, Bradford

A Monster Lurking In The Night

It is raining heavily and dark.
Gloomy!
The thunderstorm is here.
But that's when I see something very scary...
What can I see? In the shadows ahead of me?
Four red eyes, two long arms reaching for me!
Webbed feet waddling along like a duck.
Humungous mouth roaring out loud.
It is raining heavily and I can see something very scary.

Ummehani Jamshad (10)
Lady Royd Primary, Bradford

Choco

My name is Choco
I smell like Coco
I love to be happy
But never angry
I may look ugly
As I am very funny
I love to eat cake
But I hardly ever bake
My favourite colour is brown
But I hate to frown
I am never good at school
Because I am a fool
My name is Choco.

Maryam Zia (10)
Lady Royd Primary, Bradford

Cute Candy

M y very cute monster
O n top of the bed
N o one can see her
S he is kind, pretty and smells like candy
T hen in a blink of an eye, she's ferocious!
E veryone falls for her tricks
R un away before it's too late! *Beware!*

Hannah Ali (10)
Lady Royd Primary, Bradford

Charmander

It's small but strong
And its tail is long,
Mess about with horns on his head
And you'll be dead,
It may be cute but don't let that fool you,
If you hurt it'll hurt you!
You can befriend it by making its tail lit,
It may seem bad but it can be your lad!

Aaban Nawaz (10)
Lady Royd Primary, Bradford

My Monster

My monster is ten years old
His name is Money
He loves techy stuff
Loves helping people
He's cute and loves fruit
He is also scary and hairy and fluffy
He's like a mother hen being respectful
He loves making memories
He is stealthy and healthy.

Mr Shayan (13)
Lady Royd Primary, Bradford

Slimy Sam

Hi, my name is Slimy Sam
And if you're asking, yes I am a man.
I am very scary just like Bloody Mary, I am ugly,
But I'm also very snuggly.
I am very blue but I always go to the loo!
I am:
- **S** illy
- **A** wkward
- **M** ischievous.

Jennah Ahmed (10)
Lady Royd Primary, Bradford

Monster Shine

Hi, my name is Shine
I shine like a dime
Up in the sky all around the time
Even though my life turns around when the moon comes and takes my place
In the sky I'm always kind
When people always take photos of me.

Hafsah Khokhar (9)
Lady Royd Primary, Bradford

Monster Cheetah

My monster is fuzzy
When he washes his hair he becomes frizzy
Some people think he is cute
But to me, he is a hoot.

Muhammad Shoaban (10)
Lady Royd Primary, Bradford

The Day I Met A Monster

I got up this morning doubting the school day,
It should have been hot, it's the middle of May.
I saw a monster, as I rolled over on my side,
I was scared and ready to hide.
I got dressed although he was staring at me,
The next minute he was as green as a pea.
I thought it'd be cool if he came to school,
Although he'd better not act like a fool.
I showed him around and he fell to the ground.
I said we had science class,
He laughed and told me his mass.
We walked into class and the teacher asked,
"Monster, what's your name?"
"Jeffy Jr," he said while looking lame.
I sat and started to make a potion,
And what was my monster doing?
Running around his desk in slow motion.
So that was it, this day in May,
It has been very special, I have to say.
He sat at his desk, acted like a fool,
That's the last time I'm taking this monster to school.

Tommy Holland-Bass (9)
Lea St Mary's Catholic Primary School, Preston

The Day I Brought My Monster To School

I woke up at night and heard a little sigh
Then I heard scratching and then talking started
I saw two eyes but instead I went back to bed
When I woke up I brought her to school
And I saw two red eyeholes
And it was a monster asleep in a bed
The bed was small, so was my school
I went on the bus
Everybody looked at me
I asked the monster, "Do you have any friends?"
"I have one called Jess, she is a mess
And one called Cole, he gets coal for Christmas"
When I got to school I went red
So I got my friend called Ted
And said, "Never mind, Scarlette my monster"
I said, "Come on."
My teacher said, "Go and sit with Bobby and Robby"
My teacher went red so everybody went red

I was in detention with no attention
Scarlette saved the day while I lay down
We escaped and went to the town.

Jessica Simpson (7)
Lea St Mary's Catholic Primary School, Preston

The Day I Brought My Monster To School

Last night there was a huge storm,
I tried but all of a sudden I didn't feel warm,
I snuggled in my bed but out of my window, I saw a red light form.
I pulled my bed cover so tight I heard it tear,
I woke in the morning with a new bed cover,
It turned to me and said, "My hand feels like rubber."
I jumped out of bed and screamed,
He told me not to worry as he only ate cream.
I got changed into my uniform and went down to the bus,
He made a lot of fuss.
A few hours later we went down to lunch,
I asked for brunch,
All Blade wanted to do was munch.
As the end of the school day came,
Blade didn't take any blame.
He sat in class with a pencil in his hand,
He said, "This is a lovely piece of land."

But at the end of the day,
He wanted to stay in my bag until May.

Eden Heslop (9)
Lea St Mary's Catholic Primary School, Preston

The Day Monster Went To School

Today I woke up for school
And saw a monster playing with a tool.
He looked at me and I looked at him
And then said, "You're a fool!"
He looked at me and I looked at him,
I knew he wanted to play but the month is May.
I asked him to come to school,
He said yes but only with his friend Jess.
We got in the car and started to zoom
And then he said, "Where is Boom?"
We got to school and he still had his tool
And said, "Can I fix the wall?"
I said, "No," and he said, "Why Joe?"
We got to class, he started his sheet very neat.
But then he did a big bang and sang.
The teacher got mad and he got sad
And the monster got kicked out of the room
And assumed he got moved
And that's the last time Monster is going to school!

Joe O'Donnell (7)
Lea St Mary's Catholic Primary School, Preston

The Day I Met A Monster

I woke up in the morning and went to get dressed
I found my dress and Dad said it was a mess
And something furry was under my bed
I went over and pulled it out
It was a monster all hairy and brown
I had a chat, it turned out it had a cat
I decided to take her to school
My science teacher thought she was really cool
I went into history and Miss Flower was mad
As I had brought a monster into her class
She tried to get Scarrlet off me
But she disappeared in a flash
I thought my day with my monster had ended
But there was nothing I could do but go to singing class
But when I got there Scarrlet was there
Miss Bennet didn't mind
So I was allowed my monster back
Just for tonight, how kind.

Nabila Malek (8)
Lea St Mary's Catholic Primary School, Preston

The Day I Had A Friend

In the middle of the night, I heard a thump
So I didn't dare to move a lump
I was going downstairs and then I looked in the cupboard
But I couldn't see anything so I went back to bed
Then I felt like something was under my bed.

Then I looked under my bed
Then I saw something red and green
And it looked like a tail
But it was flashing with sparks
So I got dressed then I felt stressed
Then I saw a monster
So I said to him, "What is your name?"
"My name is Spane"
Then we got a rope and went to the pope.

Fun fact about my monster
If he gets scared he will shoot red hot lasers out of his eyes.

Darcey Rose Chambers (8)
Lea St Mary's Catholic Primary School, Preston

Escape Scrap Rapper!

One day I went to the park
But the bin was moving
Suddenly, the bin fell over and a can popped out
shaped like a hand
Then a monster tried to get me
So I ran out of... ahh... a bee!

Yesterday was scary, I saw a monster
But I just saw it in the window looking sharper
And while I was on the school bus
I saw him acting sus.

When I was at school I named him Scrap Rapper
Because he looked like ripped-up scrap paper
He was being very naughty
So I said, "Let's go walky."

We finally got back
With my backpack
The monster went to his home
And that's the end of my poem!

Leos Koutsokostas (7)
Lea St Mary's Catholic Primary School, Preston

A Monster Plan To Take Over Earth

When I woke up for school
I saw a monster in the swimming pool
He stared at me really hard
He was holding a piece of card
Then he disappeared and was gone for a year
The monster planned to take over the world
In his lab, he had an army
While eating a Smartie
Playing on his Nintendo Switch
Playing Super Mario fighting Wario
The monster threw a bomb at the city
And then covered it with goop
Calling in an army troop
The world was covered with monsters
And humans went extinct.

Noah Foxall-Holmes (9)
Lea St Mary's Catholic Primary School, Preston

I Took My Monster To School

One day, I was sleeping
I heard a crash and a flash and a bash
In the middle of the night
I woke up at ten o'clock in the morning
I rolled out of bed and I saw Sweetie the monster
She said she wanted jelly
I got her some jelly and took her to school
She listened for a bit
Until I saw her upside down eating jelly
And she said it was fun.

Maisie Lawson (7)
Lea St Mary's Catholic Primary School, Preston

My Monster

My monster went out to play
And I watched with glee while I started to wee
And I saw my monster staring at me

While I was playing I was saving the ball
While my monster kicked the ball
I went up my neighbour's wall.

Isla Rose Penrington (8)
Lea St Mary's Catholic Primary School, Preston

The Day I Took A Monster To School

Yesterday there was a crash,
It happened in a flash.
When I got in bed,
I squeezed my teddy,
And snuggled my pillow.

As the next day arrived,
I took a dive in the bath,
While solving a hard maths question.

Agatha Holmes (8)
Lea St Mary's Catholic Primary School, Preston

Monster On The Plane

One day I woke up to play
For some reason
I saw a monster shaped like a monster
That was not like a lobster
The monster started to play every day.

Deondre Thompson (8)
Lea St Mary's Catholic Primary School, Preston

Bobby's Adventure

On the way back from school I met Bobby.
Bobby is a monster.
He is only two foot three.
He is quite a scary but smiley monster.
Bobby is as green as slime.
He said he was on an aircraft but it crashed.
Bobby said he didn't know how to get back.
Neither did I, but then I knew...
"I know!" I screamed.
"A rocket is taking off tonight at midnight.
We can go tonight!"
So we went on the stroke of midnight.
I helped Bobby sneak into the rocket and we said our goodbyes.
"I hope we see each other again," said Bobby.
"Me too," I said.
"I forgot to tell you!" Bobby said.
"I've got some friends on Pluto.
And I'll tell them all about you."

Violet Williams (8)
Llangan Primary School, Bridgend

Mr Potato 2.0

Once there was a potato in a supermarket and it came to life.
It ran onto the street and a person picked the potato up and said, "Are you alive?"
The person was very scared.
"I am! I just came alive."
"Okay, potato, I think you should be called Mr Potato 2.0," said the person.
"Okay, person, what is your name?"
"Person? My name is Rosey.
Let us go to my house, Mr. Potato by the 2.0,
And I will let you live here for a bit,
But then you will have to go."
"Okay, Rosey," said Mr. Potato 2.0.

"I am a news reporter. I forgot to tell you.
Can I tell the world about you?" said Rosey.
Mr Potato said, "Will I be famous?"
"Yes," said Rosey.
So, Rosey talked to the whole world about him.
Everyone was talking about him
And how he had the potential to be a superhero.

That day there was a meteor coming to Earth,
So Mr Potato jumped in a space rocket and flew to the meteor.
But he was alive because he got away in an escape pod and saved the world.

James King
Llangan Primary School, Bridgend

The Eight Elemental Ohio Beast

Once upon a time,
There was a boy called Ethan, also known as me.
I saw on the TV that two monsters were found in Ohio.
So, I hopped in my car and headed to Ohio.
I saw the depths of Ohio, it was surprisingly dark.
But then something caught my eye,
Then I leapt over the border,
But I tried going back but I couldn't leave.
I realised that the thing that caught my eye was an egg.
I started to slowly creep up to the egg
And to my surprise, I heard rumbling.
It was the mother!
It was chasing me so fast, super-fast!
He looked beastly,
He had Venus fly traps in one of his hands
And a deadly weapon in the other.
He suddenly collapsed, and then he was calling,
And I saw an army of them!

I ran as fast as I could!
Along the way, he was destroying the Earth,
Killing innocent citizens with it,
My family and I were the last.
Then we saw a rocket and off we flew,
Fluttering into the sky.

Ethan Porter (9)
Llangan Primary School, Bridgend

Sparky Strikes The Earth

When I was just about to go to bed,
I lifted my head and out of the window.
I saw a sight, it was Sparky.
I saw a mythical monster
With fuzzy fur and cute, curly claws.
But when I went to stroke him, he said, "*Stop!*"
Then he said, "When you touch me,
You will just go *pop!*"
I said, "Oh, okay, I will take you to school."
So I packed my bag and left to go to school.
When I was just in the hall,
Sparky jumped out of my bag onto the wall,
Because he saw his dad, Lightning.
"How did you get here?" asked Sparky.
"One second, I was on Planet-04104
And then I teleported to wherever we are now?"
But whilst that was happening,
All of the kids were trying to stroke him.
He tried to say stop, but it was too late.
The teacher tried to take him away but... *Pop!*

She was gone, it was chaos, it was crazy and...
Bang!
They were back in their home world.

Harry King (9)
Llangan Primary School, Bridgend

The Ugly Monster

Once upon a time
There was someone called Chaotic Daisy
And Chaotic Daisy was spiky like a hedgehog
And on her head, she was soft like a sheep
She had spiky legs like sticks
And square arms and hands
She was holding signs saying
I'm Here To Scare You
And the other one said *Children*
She had big ears, like a rabbit but bigger
Lots of blood on her lips and a scary mouth
She had four eyes
Her eyes were as black as black paint
She was fierce, ugly and chaotic
She was naughty and scary
She was hairy, really hairy
She was weird and silly and stinky.

Isla Harris (8)
Llangan Primary School, Bridgend

Fuzzy Thing's New School

Once I met a new teacher,
Who was from Jupiter,
Everyone knew she was a monster.
She tried to disguise herself,
But it didn't quite work out.
So after a few days at her school,
With every child bullying her,
Like she was a killer.
She needed a break from school.
So she did.
When she came back to teach,
Everyone stopped bullying her,
For some weird reason.
The children were only being nice because,
They had an assembly about Fuzzy Thing,
Saying, be nice to Fuzzy Thing.
So everyone was.
When she saw everyone they were,
Crazily caring, and all over her,
For the rest of her career,
Until she retired from the school.

Katie Norris
Llangan Primary School, Bridgend

Roise And Her First Day Of School

Once there was a rainbow named Roise
She was as cute as a puppy
She was two feet tall and she loved people
And she was born in a forest
One day she went to school
And everybody loved her
She had one hundred friends
And one time she was playing in the yard
Then Roise changed her shape
She turned into a rock!
The children were in shock!
When the bell rang back in the class she was a pen
Then a child used the pen
And Roise turned back into the monster
And she said, "Boo!"
And they all lived happily ever after.

Skye Mordecai (9)
Llangan Primary School, Bridgend

Crazy Monster

Crazy Monster was in the rain
He was running back home
He hit something hard
Thump went his leg
A big brown treasure box
It had a shiny, silver lock
The lid popped open
A tiny planet shone
A planet in a jar
Gold, shiny coins
When he touched it
He got sucked into the treasure box
He fell into a different galaxy
It was green and red
He met a bad creature and he made a black hole.
Crazy Monster made a black hole
It blew up... *Boom, crash, pow!*
Crazy Monster beat the bad creature!

George (8)
Llangan Primary School, Bridgend

Bob's Adventure

Bob came from space and space was really cool
It had lots of cool colours
And Bob did not like children
Bob was as blue as the sky
And he saw other monsters
And they were scary, slimy, spooky monsters
And Bob was a dangerous, crazy, evil monster
One day he went to school
And he packed his bag ready for school
And he went to school
Bob met Pompom
And they were best friends with Pompom
And they were best friends forever
And they went on lots of adventures together.

Marla O'Connor (8)
Llangan Primary School, Bridgend

Fluffy At The Beach

When I was at the beach,
I saw a beautiful monster,
She was sitting on a rock,
In the middle of the sea,
I swam to the rock,
I asked her, "What is your name?"
She said, "I'm Fluffy,"
And I said, "My name is Sophie,
I have black hair as dark as the night sky,
Come and play on the sand with me,
I will keep you safe,
I will bake you a cake,
That I will make,
You will be my cute, colourful,
Clever monster forever."

Sophie Egan (8)
Llangan Primary School, Bridgend

Jeremy The Monster

It was Bob's brilliant birthday
He got the perfect pet
Jeremy the monster
As fiery as the sun
Jeremy and Bob were having lots of fun
They went on a walk
They met Evil Pork
The horrid pig
Who trapped Bob in a wooden pit
Jeremy shot fire out of his eyes
And gave Evil Pork a really bad surprise
He saved Bob
And called his friend Rob
To destroy Evil Pork
The whole town thanked him
For defeating that pork dork.

Toby Bates (9)
Llangan Primary School, Bridgend

Joy Explores School

I am Joy,
I was born in Sad Land but I want to travel
To somewhere called Happy Land.
I am as green as green grass.
I would love to go to school
But would go to Happy Land.
What? I have an idea.
I will go to travel and find a school at Happy Land.
I am jumping with happiness at the thought of school.
In real life, I find a school in Happy Land.
"Hurray!" I cheer and I make more friends.

Gracie Griffiths
Llangan Primary School, Bridgend

Swirly And The Underminer

Once upon a time
There was a girl who loved rainbows.
And then there was a sound
Bang, crash, thud!
She said, "Who is shaking the ground?
Let's investigate!
It is coming from underground
I think I know...
The Underminer"
Swirly went underground.
Underground it was dark and moody.
Spiders were crawling on the ground.
Swirly was brave and strong.

Georgiana Dando
Llangan Primary School, Bridgend

Crazy Crackers

Once upon a time, there was a monster.
This monster was called Crackers.
This monster once was a boy.
But he got turned into a monster by being bitten by a chicken and then eating a crispy cracker.
That's why he was a cracker with chicken legs.
The monster was from Ohio.
And we went there on a holiday and the monster nearly took over the world.
But before he did, Mr Potato 2.0 had saved the world.

Dylan O'Connor (9)
Llangan Primary School, Bridgend

Joey The Shapeshifter

Once upon a time,
There was a person called Joey the Shapeshifter.
He could change into anything he wanted to.
He was eight foot four.
He was a spy disguised as a poor man.
Started going around people's houses to get money.
It didn't work because a person ripped off his mask.
The police came to the house and he got put in jail.
Joey cried as he got put in jail, never to be seen again.

Mollie Griffiths
Llangan Primary School, Bridgend

Monster Poetry - Creepy Creations

Pom Pom's Story Of Life

Pom Pom came from a forest
The forest was light and bright
An egg rolled down the hill
That led from the forest
The egg hit a rock
Crack went the egg
And Pom Pom popped out of the egg
Pom Pom was as yellow as the sun and very cute
She went to monster school
And met Bob and they were best friends forever
And they went on lots of adventures together.

Scarlett Powell-Bright (8)
Llangan Primary School, Bridgend

Penny The Buff Dog

Penny was a normal dog until a space rock hit her.
But when Penny was hit,
She became as blue as the ocean.
She was a blue, buff Bowser of a dog.
Penny started to protect her owner.
One time, bored of fighting, tired all the time,
Killer Spook flew away,
Fast like a jet booming across the sky.

Noah Williams (8)
Llangan Primary School, Bridgend

Monster

Phieus the Monster
Was off for a walk
On a bright sunny day
Walking his alien dog
On the green grass
Philis was as scared
As a monster
Home he ran
Slam went the door
He needed a cup of tea
And monster biscuits.

Ruby Hill (8)
Llangan Primary School, Bridgend

Red Spice Journey

Red Spice was born in an erupting volcano,
His water brother was wet as a wave,
And they had a fight all day,
And Red Spice was tired out,
Something was happening,
He became scary, slimy, and scaly,
And Red Spice won.

Jack Stevens (8)
Llangan Primary School, Bridgend

Tom The Monster

Tom was a fluffy blue monster
He went to school
To learn about the demolition monster
He was not afraid
Strong and tough
Tom was as friendly as a cat
But wasn't afraid to fight
So, he went to defeat him.

Bailey Williams (8)
Llangan Primary School, Bridgend

The Killer

He was from a haunted village!
He was as blue as the sky.
He was a scary, slimy, and spooky monster.
But then Penny came and battled him.
But then he got bored and ran away.
Never to be seen again.

Isaac Edwards (8)
Llangan Primary School, Bridgend

Cracked

Whilst I was walking across the beach,
A monster that looked like an egg rolled past me.
As I was running after it,
I was calling its name, "Cracked, Cracked, Cracked."
Finally, it calmed down and came to me.
Then I noticed it had three small spectral eyes as small as fifteen little specks.

"I want to go in the sea," I said.
But it was so hot that he started boiling when he got in,
So we just got out straight away.
After all that, he started rolling away into a fish and chips shop.
He said he wanted some fish so I bought him some.

After, we went to his house and watched some TV.
We also did some talking with each other.
I said, "Today's been great."
He said, "Are you sure about that?"
And then he ate me.

Rocco Staples (8)
Long Whatton CE Primary School, Loughborough

Kity The Queen

I.
A proud family moved from a house,
Into a decent temple,
Dangerously close to a cliff,
Afare not so a black sea pondered,
Sea salt filled the air like perfume,
Not knowing what was lurking,
Was a mistake so wrong,
A secret was here.

II.
The family entered,
The priests were mad,
As the temple was holy,
Soon no more,
The priests were bribed,
To ban the spirits,
Clean out corpses,
Buried so long.

III.
Throughout the night soft purrs were heard,
This enraged the mother,
Telling her love,
"Find the source of the noise,"
He searched,
He found,
But a small ginger kitten,
Eyes like fire,
But meowing in pain,
He tended the wound,
Fond he became,
Feeding and stroking,
His love was in vain,
He did not know what creature desired,
A ball was hosted,
A girl appeared,
In silk and velvet,
Caught the eyes of many,
But she danced with one fair-haired man,
She danced gracefully,
As if love waltzed her way.

IV.
Soon it finished,
No more music playing in heads,
The people left,
The only ones left,
Were the girl and a different man,
And a family who hosted,
Soon the cat returned,
Supposedly the music scared her off,
But that is a question only she could answer.

Edith Macfarlane (9)
Long Whatton CE Primary School, Loughborough

All About Lavish Logan

In a Lamborghini,
Logan lands from the magic moon on elderly Earth
With a clash, slash and smash.
He has beady, brown eyes
And crazy, curly hair.
He isn't a hero yet
And has zero enemies.
But he doesn't like aggressive animals.
And aggressive animals are his biggest fear,
For you can hear him secretly scared.
But he does like cute cats and funny fish.
He is really rich with a luxurious Lamborghini and a fast Ferrari.
His mum was a hopeful heptathlete and is now a famous, courageous coach.
And his dad is a famous coach who coaches famous people
In fun football, realistic rugby, amazing athletics
And loads of different sports.
So we know that Logan has had a fantastic eight years
And will have an amazing time for the rest of his life.

Logan Dodoo (8)
Long Whatton CE Primary School, Loughborough

Demon To The Moon

The six-eyed monster wanted the moon,
He was getting hungry, so he decided to move,
He fell from hell, when he saw the moon,
That's when he decided to destroy it.

The monster needed to travel,
Luckily, he had a pitchfork and an axe,
They both had rocket boosters to fly him up,
With his horns, he could dig into the moon.

The monster started flying,
Soon he reached the moon,
When he dug in it felt all squishy,
So he climbed to the top.

On the moon, he started to eat,
And realised it was cheese,
He started eating more,
Until half the moon was gone.

Now he's charged up,
He can take over the world,

He flew back down,
To explode the Earth.

He hovered over Earth,
Then dropped ten bombs,
The world started to explode,
He dropped one last bomb.

But then the bomb flew behind him,
It came roaring down from behind,
It hit him,
It exploded,
He died,
The world was recreated,
Everyone was ecstatic.

Keigan Fearn (8)
Long Whatton CE Primary School, Loughborough

Eerie Fighter

A monster came to school,
Our first class was in the pool,
He walked into the darkest corner,
And turned into a sparkling, shimmering salmon,
He swam, and swam, and swam,
Without making a splash,
He turned back to a flying monster,
But flew away in a dash.

A creature came to school,
It gobbled up a sandwich,
While I tongued his language,
He then did a burp,
Which made the other children gasp for breath,
Then wiped his mouth with a tablecloth,
And walked out slowly like a sloth.

A friendly monster came to school,
Our last class was art,
The silly monster painted on the wall,
He painted a steaming, hot tart,
He then went crazy,

He painted on everyone,
Covered in sticky paint, everybody left,
Leaving the miserable monster bowing his head,
We were walking back home,
He vanished,
All that was left... was his name.

Tessa Bradley (8)
Long Whatton CE Primary School, Loughborough

The Fluffy Friend

Today the new Receptions joined the school.
I'm going to show Pete around now.
"Hello Pete, I'm going to show you around school today!
Wait, you have wings, can you fly?"
"Yes."

"Do you want to see the playground first today?"
"Okay."
"Here is the climbing wall.
Put your leg on there, your arm on there,
Your leg there and lastly put your arm there.
Hooray, you're up.
Okay, next, the hall.
You eat all your meals there,
Sometimes you have a disco.
Okay, next is the toilets, they do smell,
This is where you do your stuff."

Okay, the fluffy friend is now in Year Six
And is showing Andy around.

"Wait a minute, you're a monster like me."
"I feel good for him," said me in Year Twelve.

Thomas Robertshaw (9)
Long Whatton CE Primary School, Loughborough

New Mermaid School

Once a upon time under the sea,
Was a girl called Catgirl,
Catgirl was going to mermaid school,
So Catgirl was cool,
Catgirl said trim, skim, slum, shim,
But Catgirl was brave and behaved.

They had a disco in the school,
Catgirl was a rainbow mermaid,
A girl said, "You look cool,"
Catgirl said, "Thank you,"
A boy said, "Do you like the disco?"
"Yes," said Catgirl.

A naughty girl said, "She's not cool at all,"
Catgirl was sad because she was not cool,
A girl came up and said, "She's just being silly."

It was Catgirl's birthday,
The teacher said, "Happy birthday Catgirl!"

Lauren Winter (8)
Long Whatton CE Primary School, Loughborough

Dave The Drumming Dragon

Green fur, and blue polka dot spots,
Blue eyes, he likes pies,
Pukka pies to be *precise*,
He loves to play drums in fact,
Play all day and night,
But not like any other monsters, he hates to fight.

Dave was a dangerous drummer,
His sticks were nylon tipped,
He liked to lick his sticks before a gig,
People said he was a monster round the kit,
In the studio he loved to jam,
Rock and rumble,
He never tumbled over the kit,
He still loves to lick his sticks,
His moves around the kit are slick.

Dave the Drumming Dragon.

Billy Steel (9)
Long Whatton CE Primary School, Loughborough

The Monster's Adventure

One day the monster landed in a weird place,
He tried to talk to people but they spoke a different language,
So he went to the shop but he was shy,
So he stole something.

Then he tried to figure out where he was in Italy in Rome,
So he went to see Roman things and the stone houses,
He found an English person and he got a flight home.

And he went to school then he did maths then reading,
And then it was home time,
He went in his rocket ship home.

Then he had dinner, then he went to bed.

Joshua Bown (8)
Long Whatton CE Primary School, Loughborough

Hyrule's New King

A dragon called Uphevil wanted to be king,
Instead he was a guard,
Protecting King Ganon from danger,
You could say he was scarred.

Until Ganon asked him for a chat,
Which was today,
He prepared a plan,
Hip hip hooray!

The chat went on for hours,
Then Uphevil made his move,
His move was powerful,
Because if Ganon was alive,
He would disapprove.

Ganon is dead,
Uphevil is king,
Now his objective is,
To give Link a big sting!

Jack Mayfield (9)
Long Whatton CE Primary School, Loughborough

Fuzz

A pup landed in London.
She has one olive green eye.
With a sky blue fuzzy coat.
An emerald colour.
Her owner's name is Trubble.
She is purple with a jet pack.

She is still in London with nothing to do.
Let's go to the art gallery.
See what we can do.
A picture of fuzz.
Hanging on the wall.

Now she's all tired and sleepy.
She has to go to bed.
I hear her barking in my sleep.
Maybe it was just a dream.

Izzy Mantey (8)
Long Whatton CE Primary School, Loughborough

A Dragon Destroying The Universe

The three-headed, midnight-black dragon,
Had an evil plan to destroy the universe,
It had swirly wings,
A cross-hatch body,
Blood-red eyes,
The aggressive dragon,
Three spikes on each head,
Is a dangerous dragon...

Up, up, up it flies,
Lands in Russia,
Everyone cries,
Eventually ruling over the world,
It invades the planets and dwarf planets,
"The world is mine,
Dragons and aliens rule the universe."

Maisy Chadaway (9)
Long Whatton CE Primary School, Loughborough

The Dancing Daisy

A four-eyed creature landed in London.
Her wings were calming and wavy like the sea.
She used her wings to fly to the top of an eye of a tower.
Because the Grand Flower was opening,
And it sold the best monster clothes.
Finally, it opened,
And my monster and I went to buy some clothes.
We got a top and got a new prop, to go in our kitchen.
In our house, we've got a pet mouse.
After we did our shopping, we went home and went to bed.

Harper Bowley (8)
Long Whatton CE Primary School, Loughborough

Raidius

Raidius is a magma salamander,
It was born in a meteor.

There's a new monster in school,
Its marble claws glimmer in the moon,
Its eyes are as dark as coal burning,
It smells for vengeance against anyone that's daring.

The new monster in school,
Was found in the corner looking rather cool,
Whatever he touched turned into ashes,
The teachers were scared of his tears because he cried out acid.

Oliver Claye (8)
Long Whatton CE Primary School, Loughborough

Shadows

Daylight turns to night,
While the moonlight gets brighter,
When the moonlight is complete,
A creature lurks and creeps,
It peeks out from its hiding place,
And jumps up on its feet,
It pounces at the nearest person,
And rips them apart from top to bottom.

Run away, shout and cry,
The ones who face it will scream and die,
And if it uses its special power,
You will turn to ice and be devoured.

Nate Sharples (9)
Long Whatton CE Primary School, Loughborough

The Monster Mermaid

The monster mermaid landed in the sea
The monster mermaid saw a poster on the bridge
A Dog Missing!
Then the monster turned into a mermaid!
She said, "What's going on?
A merdog on the bridge?
What the..."
And the monster's dog was called Lother
She could fetch the ball
So fast for the monster mermaid
And she could do a front flip.

Lily Winter (8)
Long Whatton CE Primary School, Loughborough

The Three-Headed Dog

The three-headed dog is very dangerous,
She has vibrant, green eyes,
She lived on a planet with lots of other monsters in her world,
But she appeared in a crash, smash, bash,
She appeared from a cloud of smoke,
I start to pet her, she is very soft and fluffy,
But she is giant with black fur,
But has two scars on her!
Off we go on a walk, but she needs a collar.

Evie Claye (8)
Long Whatton CE Primary School, Loughborough

The Apocalypse

A snake eating everything,
Buying JCBs,
Driving to Liverpool,
Left right,
Left right.

The apocalypse is near!
Exploding towns,
With pineapples,
While eating vine apples,
He cries for his allies.

Death is near,
Everyone screams
At this beast.
The people are infuriated -
Hated is the great devourer.

Tom Gaskell (8)
Long Whatton CE Primary School, Loughborough

Candyfloss' First School Day

It's time for school now, don't be late,
You'll meet Dora, Scooby-Doo, and Pete,
Keep your drawer nice and neat,
Don't forget your lunch box,
And money for the shop.

I'm off to school, don't be late,
Hip hip hooray, it's so cool.

Layla Biddulph (8)
Long Whatton CE Primary School, Loughborough

Fluffee

Fluffee goes on an adventure
She has gone to America
She is excited
She is cuddly like a teddy bear
She stays in a hotel that has posh stuff
She is very nice and cute.

Lilah Afonso (8)
Long Whatton CE Primary School, Loughborough

Fiery Freddie

I was in a forbidden cave
When I looked around the corner and saw it
Its skin was molten red
With volcano particles flying off him.

It had an expensive-looking top hat
I'm not too sure what to think about that
It had massive, dragon-like wings
And on those wings were a few rings.

I slowly approached it with a nervous walk
And suddenly it began to talk
"Hello," it said, "my name is Fiery Fred."

He told me a story all about his evil twin brother
And that he wanted to stop him from going any further
His evil twin brother was planning on destroying the world
By brainwashing us all
It was our time to destroy this fool.

Freddie showed me his breathtaking ship
And wasting no time we launched into space
Travelling at the speed of light
We got there in no time
We got to his lair with just ten minutes to spare.

Freddie and I rushed in
Then destroyed him and his stupid machine
Then we flew away back to the cave
Knowing that we saved the day.

Casey Elam (10)
Longmeadow Primary School, Broadwater

I Met A Monster On World Ocean Day

Sitting bolt upright in my bed.
I bumped my head.
I heard an unusual noise.
I went to investigate but there was nothing there.
Trying to drift back off to sleep.
But first I had a peek outside my window.
A lonely lion was on my swings!

I tiptoed into my garden and what did I see?
A lion-headed monster looking at me!

He told me, sadly, how many plastic bottles he found.
I told him we could help.
We went to the recycling bins.
We made a robot machine called Silly Sucker.
We went to our local beach and river.
In total, we had three bags of rubbish!

Then Larry told me something amazing.

He said on every World Ocean Day he flies from the sky
And helps the Earth by picking up litter.
Now we always do it together.

Indi Hyde (10)
Longmeadow Primary School, Broadwater

Barry's Chessington Adventure

Waiting for Chessington to open
I saw something blue
Falling from the sky there was a crash
Everyone turned as it went smash
There stood bright blue
A monster dressed so new
It swiped its diamond-tipped tail over its tie
And asked if they could go on a ride
They looked alone so I bought them a ticket
When Chessington opened we were the quickest
We got on the ride
A trip through the zoo
He got excited, I was surprised he wasn't frightened
Then the shock came, he fell out the car
That's not the ride
He talked to the animal
Then got confused when they didn't respond
He said I'm Barry Barrel
So that was his name

I called him back before he could touch the mane
Fortunately he was safe climbing back in
We finished the ride
He didn't look so new
During the ride he got covered in *poo*
Barry the blue dude
I'm going to see him again soon
Added to my basket some safety helmets
So I won't have to go
Phew!

Phoebe D (10)
Longmeadow Primary School, Broadwater

The Time I Met My New Friend

I was about to go to bed but all of a sudden I heard a loud crash!
In a heartbeat, I stood up.

I went downstairs to investigate what made that loud crash.
Then I started to hear loud chomping.
I was hesitant at first but eventually, I built up the courage to look around.
I saw a little winged creature eating my snacks,
When I confronted it, I saw its face,
There was chocolate all over the place.

It was a dragon!
This little dragon was in a sugar rush.
He was bouncing off the walls.
Literally.
I tried to catch it but I guess it just fell asleep.
"If someone gets a sugar rush,
They always have a sugar crash," I said,
Dragging him to my sofa.

The next day we got to properly introduce ourselves.
"Hello, my name is Mimi, which is Chinese for secret.
My name represents the secretive side to the the dragon race."

I realised he was not the only one.

Juan Ibe (10)
Longmeadow Primary School, Broadwater

The Forgotten Park...

Whilst going on a run I came across a park
Though I should go home, it was getting dark
I went in anyway just for a peek
Promised myself that when I got home
I'd go back to sleep.

I saw a willow tree
It looked fascinating to me
That was until it moved
I saw scales and fins
A fish-type thing.

I finally uncovered
The secrets of the forgotten park
I went on my way
But she begged me to stay
And we are still friends
Up to this day.

Mia-Lily Whitfield (10)
Longmeadow Primary School, Broadwater

Bread

My monster is from the planet Heck.
We went for ice cream, it dripped down our necks.
He smiled at me with his millions of white teeth.
His dark black eyes never blinked.

We cleaned ourselves up.
Then we went to the mall.
We didn't mean to stall.
After that, we went back.

I hope the monster will come back.
He promised.
After all, you can't break a promise.
Mum looks at me strangely.
I smile at her with my millions of white teeth.
And dark black eyes that never blink.

Sienna M (10)
Longmeadow Primary School, Broadwater

Beverley

I was cleaning my living room with my sister.
I saw something move, it was blue and six foot two.
I was scared at first as well as shocked,
Not knowing what to say or do.

I was thinking and thinking about what to do.
It had black button eyes and silver spikes all over.
It circled around my body and said, "*Boo!*"

Spiriting across the other side of the living room,
Breathing heavily,
She said her name was called Beverley.
My sister said, "Go tell Mum, this is really not fun."

I told my sister to not worry 'cause the creature was oddly friendly.
Surely it wouldn't want to hurt us?
She probably had no friends and wanted us to play.
We went to the park together and we wanted to stay all day.

We all had so much fun
And that was our day done.
She said she would visit soon at noon.

Jazzy Joseph (10)
Longmeadow Primary School, Broadwater

Ben

I was cleaning my room because we had guests
I finished everything except for the bed
I was sure I had seen something moving under the covers
I thought it was Hustle my hamster
I called out to her but all I heard was a grumble.

I checked and it was a monster that was four foot two!
I asked, "What are you doing here, you?"
She said, "I came for Ben. My friend.
I came here but I can't find him anywhere!"
"Don't worry, we will find him in a hurry!"
So we checked and checked and checked
Sorry monster, you have to go.

We heard a noise
So I checked and found blooming Ben!
She glared with excitement and thanked me again
She went back to her planet and I never saw her again.

Patricia Chiaga (10)
Longmeadow Primary School, Broadwater

The Day I Met Drandorle

In the water at the beach,
I heard something screech.
I checked underwater and something moved
It was blue and six foot two.
I saw a flame burst from the water
People left because it might've been a slaughter.
I went in and asked its name,
"Drandorle," it said, "I think it's time for bed"
"For you?" I asked
"Yes, indeed," she replied
"I failed my mission to stop pollution!"
Drandorle said, so dramatically
"Please don't go, I'll help you so,
I'll clean the beach in one sweep
Your slimy skin will be nice and neat."
"Thank you and now goodbye," Drandorle replied
"Goodbye," I sighed.

Victoria P (9)
Longmeadow Primary School, Broadwater

Snagonmaximus

I woke from a bang downstairs
I went to investigate
It was a monster, he was blue
And was about nineteen foot two!
I was terrified and was scared
I thought to myself, *what should I do?*

He spoke, "Please don't hurt me, I'm Snagonmaximus."
I asked, "Why are you here?"
He replied by telling me about his journey
He was flying to the ocean but got hurt and fell down to Earth.

We became friends and had a great day together
He took me back home and he went back into the ocean
I ran into Barry Barrel and Skwelldolop
We had a chat.

That night, I fell asleep thinking what a wonderful day I had.

Ronnie Hull (10)
Longmeadow Primary School, Broadwater

The Day A Monster Came To Visit

One Thursday morning
I was on my way to the park
When I heard a noise
It was coming from under the slide
All of a sudden
A sweet little creature popped out.

I spoke to the creature in a soft, subtle tone
Hoping it was friendly
But maybe wanted to be left alone
She only spoke a little bit of English
Mostly it was gibberish.

All I understood was that she failed her mission
Helping kids!
Without me, they would be nothing
Seeing their sweet little faces, oh, how adorable
I asked her name
Mrs Furtastic Furball.

Lacey Bradshaw (10)
Longmeadow Primary School, Broadwater

Monster Who Fell From Space

I was doing my washing
When I heard a loud smash
I decided to see what it was.

A cute creature (that looked like a panda)
I took the creature home and gave it an apple
But it ate it in one bite!
It started talking more and more and more
I gave it three more apples
Then I heard a knock on the door
It was my parents!

I ran upstairs
Hid the creature under the bed
Put a blanket over him
I ran downstairs and opened the door
"Hi Mum, hi Dad," I said quickly with my face all red
And I ran back upstairs.

Maja D (10)
Longmeadow Primary School, Broadwater

Tilly Tentacles

At the water's edge, at the beach
I saw something quite unique
It was all blue
I had no clue.

I was scared at first
Then it said, "I'm lonely, oh, won't you play with me?"
"Okay"
Then we were on our way
"Let's go to the park"
"Yes," came the reply
"Oh, and by the way, my name is Tilly Tentacles."

I still can't believe my luck
In the afternoon I knew I had to go
Go and leave that slimy serpent
I hope to see her again soon.

Lara Senior (10)
Longmeadow Primary School, Broadwater

The Day I Met A Monster

On the way back home from school
I saw a bush rustling
I was going to go check out what was in there
But before I got there a monster jumped out!

I chased him to see that he was okay
He might have got prickled by all the branches
By the time I got to him, I was lost in a frosty forest
I didn't want to take any chances.

We headed back home
But up ahead
The monster was walking, just ahead
We checked that he was okay
He dived back into the bush.

Riley Bartlett (10)
Longmeadow Primary School, Broadwater

The Ghost Of The Cave

I was hiking one day
When I entered a cave
I saw a monster
All white and grey
I fell over in shock
But he saved me from death.

We had some biscuits and tea
Then we went to the shops
He told me he held a gem.

A slimy monster tried to steal the gem
Slimy said, "Ghosty, give it to me"
Ghosty wouldn't give the gem up
We worked together and Slimy slid away.

It was time to go
We will always be best friends.

Amariah Williams (9)
Longmeadow Primary School, Broadwater

Zoe Zoo At Your Service

One day me and my family went to the zoo
Out of nowhere, a monster appeared
They said, "Oh, why hello, this is for you"
Pulling out a golden coin from their pocket.

Zoe Zoo at your service
She looked a little nervous
Shy eyes which are as blue as the sky.

I took the gold coin straight to the shop
Picked up a key chain that looked familiar
Zoe Zoo was staring up at me
I smiled as I paid for my purchase
Today was a good day.

Evie Gray (9)
Longmeadow Primary School, Broadwater

Mr Rainbow Rain

I woke up with a jolt
Because I heard a bang
So I went outside to investigate
And I saw Mr Rainbow.

He is a creature as colourful as a rainbow
Although he was a bit shy
We went to the shops and park together.

I called him Mr Rainbow Rain
He liked it more than Mr Happy Hyde
He was from Colourland.

He took me to his land
Where we went on rollercoasters
And to the beach together
He took me back down to Earth.

Holly W (10)
Longmeadow Primary School, Broadwater

Leonard's Adventure

I was at the park
Then I saw something rustle,
I went to go see
And it was crazy,
It was three foot two,
Had seven eyes and was so slimy.

I asked for his name
And got no reply,
His green arms grabbed me,
He whispered and said, "Leonard,"
I said, "Let's go to the zoo!"
Leonard shouted, "Yay!"
And off we went,
That was the day Leonard had an adventure.

Esme B (10)
Longmeadow Primary School, Broadwater

Cute Monster Violet

I met a monster
She is the kindest monster I have ever seen
She likes to travel and fly
She has lots of friends
I was walking to the park when something crashed
I went to see it
It was Violet
She was so cuddly, cute and colourful
At six foot two
She had blue wings
Pink fur and a yellow crown
I am so happy I found her
I think we are going on a trip
To her island.

Alexis S (10)
Longmeadow Primary School, Broadwater

Pandy's Journey

On my way home
I saw something move in the park
Instantly I was scared because it was dark.

All I saw were some sort of wings
I went over
A creature was there, alone
I knew I had to care
He was about four foot two and kind of blue.

Misunderstood
That was all he was
A good friend was Pandy
We are still friends to this very day.

Mia A (10)
Longmeadow Primary School, Broadwater

Gobbledygook

Glitch laughs like a witch.
Teal laughs like a seal.
Teal likes to eat a big meal.
Glitch has a big itch.
Glitch is a snitch.
Glitch speaks gobbledygook.

They take a trip to Disneyland.
And go on a very tall ride.
It is called The Tide.
The monsters get very wet.

They sail a boat home.
Glitch plays games on her phone.

Jesseca C (10)
Longmeadow Primary School, Broadwater

The Day I Met A Monster

I was cleaning my room
With the vacuum
I saw a monster
Accidentally sucking him up.

I tried to get him out
But he was very angry
He tried to bite me
I said sorry to him
He forgave me.

He helped tidy my room
When it was tidy
We went to the local library
He had to go
We said goodbye
Hope I see you soon.

Ella D (9)
Longmeadow Primary School, Broadwater

The Day Met A New Friend

I went to the beach
I saw a cave
Red, yellow and purple eyes were staring at me.

A monster came out of its nest
Its skin was as green as a frog
Well, you're gigantic!

He wanted to come to my school
I would have to smuggle him in
He turned into mist
And followed me to my class
I made him live in the bagel hut.

Tommy T (10)
Longmeadow Primary School, Broadwater

The Day I Met A Monster

I was going to put on my beautiful boots
But a little figure crawled out of them
It was growing in size
It had me surprised.

We went outside to play football
He could shoot!
And he had an amazing boot
I asked what his name was
He said, "Yuzi"
We had fun
We are still friends to this day.

Riley Barmby (10)
Longmeadow Primary School, Broadwater

I Met A Monster

I was cleaning my bedroom
I saw something move
It was a monster
The monster was four foot three
He was red and yellow
His name was Cuddly Jack
Jack was feeling scared
Carefully I put Jack in my blue bag
We went to the park to cheer him up
We played catch until 4am
We had the best day ever.

Jude Smith (10)
Longmeadow Primary School, Broadwater

The Day My Life Changed

I was at school
When a green beast took my phone
I chased him.

We ended up in Dinosaur Land
We landed on a wriggle dionsaur
We were stuck there forever.

He showed me his room
And gave me a tour
I liked it there because it was green.

Evie-Mae L (10)
Longmeadow Primary School, Broadwater

Young Writers Information

We hope you have enjoyed reading this book – and that you will continue to in the coming years.

If you're the parent or family member of an enthusiastic poet or story writer, do visit our website **www.youngwriters.co.uk/subscribe** and sign up to receive news, competitions, writing challenges and tips, activities and much, much more! There's lots to keep budding writers motivated!

If you would like to order further copies of this book, or any of our other titles, then please give us a call or order via your online account.

Young Writers
Remus House
Coltsfoot Drive
Peterborough
PE2 9BF
(01733) 890066
info@youngwriters.co.uk

Join in the conversation!
Tips, news, giveaways and much more!

YoungWritersUK   YoungWritersCW   youngwriterscw

Scan me to watch the
Monster Poetry Video